HOLY FIRES

HENRY S. KING

LILY HENRY

Illustrated by Henry S. King

Acknowledgements

I would like to thank my siblings, A. and O.- a pair of exceptional poets- for their invaluable feedback and suggestions on my poetry. If I was really going to be the one to publish, I couldn't have built this collection- or my confidence in it- without your beautifying influence. Thank you.

Thanks also to my co-author, Lily Henry, for helping me polish the poems in this volume and for being so much fun to work with. I had no idea that I could enjoy writing like this.

HSK

My poetry begins with my roots: being born into a family that had a love affair with words, I don't think I really even had a choice but to begin writing poetry as a child, and I've never stopped.

Today, my three adult children inspire me, and my husband encourages me. My gratitude is enormous.

LH

CONTENTS

Holy Fires 1

Ada 2

Three Wounds 4

Ranges 6

Battle Song of the Dachshunds 8

Alice 10

Olivia 11

Another Poem About Spring 13

A Ratatouille of Divine Love.. 14

Apologies to My Husband 15

Before the Hysterectomy... 16

Dominic's Candle 18

Correspondence Today.. 19

Fern 22

Patter 24

Desire 26

Prairie Hymn 28

Hash Brown Elegy 29

Dominic 30

Inarticulate 34

The Day Before the Razor Blade 35

The Likeness 39

Makeshift Office... 40

Frustration in Full 41

Fern, Refashioned 42

Gratitude... 43

Staying Power 45

In the Courthouse (The Murder of Hope)............................. 46

Aftermath.. 48

Memorable Music 49

Mr. A. and Beth 50

Warm Water 51

Last/First 53

Helpless Bystander 54

Inspiration/Expiration 55

On Breathing 56

Dusk on the Patio 57

On the Verge 58

Crude 60

One 61

Veiled 64

Hurricane 65

Serenity 66

Toffee 69

Seascape 70

The Cycle 72

Moving Back to Colorado 73

Self-Inflicted Homesickness 75

He's Perfect, Thanks 76

Un/Shaken 77

Ingathering 78

Frances 79

A Very Long Wait 81

Illness, Ingrate 83

The Body That Was Broken For Us 84

Rush Hour 86

Thought for a Mountain Lake 89

The Wild City 90

My Companion 92

The One You Win by Losing 94

Two Surgeons 95

Christopher 96

Not Quite Eden, But Still 97

Firstfruits 98

A Heady Year 99

Fire Spoke For Us 100

Two-Man Angel Band 101

Keeper... 103

God with the Desperate 105

Slapdash Neighbors 106

Retention Pond Jesus... 107

Before We Met 108

Peace on Earth, Goodwill to Shoppers............................ 109

Violins 112

The Asylum Seekers 113

Bear All Things.. 114

Saltbush Lives Forever 116

Tinsel Prophet.. 118

Milk Leaps 119

Swampland 120

Guilty By Reason of Inattention...................................... 121

(Untitled) 122

The Universal Hymn.. 124

Jaelynn 125

Song of a Woman... 126

Center 128

Holy Fires

You stopped with a sudden stare
With your eyes rounded by a
Child's essential loneliness
Reflecting the still, pale
Simplicity that is still
Attaining after the bright
Riot of belated adolescence
All gaudy feathers and thorns
And now you are petrified
By the vitric stillness of
Placid civility.
And maybe you'll stop at
That one still house on the
Frozen shore and maybe
You'll stay and you'll be still,
But I think more likely
Bright riots are in your blood
And you will go back whirling
Yelping hectic Hosannas
Right back into all that glare
And all that precious glitter.

-HSK

1

Ada

You arrived,
your eyes and mouth rounded in astonishment,
uncertain of just
where you are
and what you are meant to be doing here.

You turned, but that way was closed,
the only exit the one far ahead,
beyond brambles and beggings,
fog and spirit.
Head down, breath in,
you began.

You collided with walls
you didn't see,
ran into corners that sprung up in this
strange dimension you only
half live in,
leaving you to wonder:
Am I supposed to turn here?

I have seen you listen
to the tones of Elsewhere,
that place from which you graced us,
that space to which you seem
to yearn to return,
your head cocked,
your limbs still,
you look behind you,
but that way is still closed.

Shaking yourself back into action,
you continue.

What I want to say is this:
I understand.
I know where you came from,
and I want to go back there, too.
You look around, trying to make sense
of this senselessness.
You never stop trying
You never stop going
I promise you: You will return.

We are uncertain what to do with
your beauty and that grace
that flows outward
and puzzles inward.
We hold our arms out,
hoping to support you,
to catch you,
but instead you rise back up
on your own cloud-formed feet
and you continue.

You will return.

-LH

Three Wounds

Here in the land of the dying and dead,
Coruscations draw the gaze aside-
Pardon aches that flare and then subside;
Gems are the hungers that end when they're fed.

Harder to shake what the dumb creature mind
Wants with water-wavered bliss and pain-
Petrichor and sunlight stippled rain-
Its freshness of species nostalgia refined

By the sharp edge of endings unclearly conceived,
Thus bewildered away from unwavering light.

Then at the sigh of a son misperceived
I pitied those who never lived as heirs-
Who withdrew from fields that were theirs,
Nullifying loveliness, love-bloomed and -leaved.

Is this a thorn in the crown of delight:
Lavish green presented pollen-starred-
That gracious note of love when jilted, scarred-
Spurned as a promise to hold and unite,

When behind brown Kedesh's escarpment in shame,
We recoiled from the shrapnel of shattering grace?

I want to venture a radical claim,

Driven by the jasmine bush toward fall-

Slanting morning in its leaves- in all

The sweetness and grief of the late summer flame:

Come, show to me the most courteous face,

But, when murk and guilt disperse and fade,

Stand in monuments that goodness made:

Brightest of days, with those dapples like lace.

Let the stab of sharp ecstasy, deathliness shed,

Come with faith and the daylight completely aligned.

-HSK

Ranges

Arid

Amber evening

Ranges- thunderheads in

Ambush to the east to thwart his

Riding

-HSK

Affection, Life-Long

Immortal in moral, immortal as traced with a delicate forelimb
to reanimating, cool waterlets

dewy into gasping brilliance
and
its circumference of illustrious this,

honed to a resplendent
        though frail
entity

Trip cheerfully and
until one needs to shout as tenderly as
stripped branches:
Priceless!

-LH

Battle Song of the Dachshunds

When after morning walks we find ourselves
With bellies full abandoned to the day,
Well, then it's time to gird our loins and shelve
Our cravings for more treats and sleeps, and pray
That one more day will bring us great good luck
In guarding here your precious domicile.
We stand our posts or proudly run amok
Determined that no scum will sneak in while
Your cherished sausage pups are here to slam
The windows, yap and snarl and mark the floor!
That beagle- vanquished! Barked away! A pram-
In fear it rolled right by! The bike- no more!

When you return, you'll see the rugs and sigh
With pride to know your home is safe thereby.

-HSK

Alice

unfortunate a how should

        a laugh be

a mask

a

smile be pro

tecting

        yet a

          touch

           be a

            mirror how

pessi

mystic is a bright I'd grin

(if only the glass were turned) and

the WHAT we're taught among fledgling rot

        redefined

          as the what-

           we've learned

-LH

Olivia

You're the olive branch extended to an uncertain
World, the sign of parents' audacity to grasp
At the hope of what can only be a fragile
Type of temporary peace, and call it enough
To feed the hope for golden human ages
And sufficient peace and plenty in your time.

At Olivet they heard about the heavy time
Of tribulation when their conquest seemed uncertain,
And they knew it was unknown what endless ages
Would come before the kingdom was in their grasp
And they had to take the promise of it as enough
To hold a hope that must have sometimes seemed too fragile.

In form an olive bloom looks far too fragile
To blossom over stones for any length of time,
But we've all taken it as grace enough
That if we can stumble through the mists, uncertain,
Holding hands out waiting for his ageless grasp
Savoring the prayer for light as we have for ages,

Then olive trees can likewise endure ages,
And lend their silver shade to cover fragile
Lives, the bits of breath that keep a tenuous grasp
On landscapes known for harshness, through relentless time.
Your strength is that you came to us uncertain;
We hoped your instinct for enduring was enough.

On Olivet he must have thought that nothing was enough

To keep our faith about the future ages

When we'd proved to be unendingly uncertain

Of absolution, because our works are lamely fragile.

Courteously, he showed us one final time

In spite of plagues and pains, he has us in his grasp.

Olive drab and blood are all we see within our grasp,

Sometimes, or masks and needles seem like they're not enough

To give what we demand as our full span of time,

But here we stand in the rubble of the ages,

And with us, you, all silvery and fragile,

The olive branch held out to the uncertain.

In this unsettled time, we don't know when we'll grasp

A grace that feels uncertain, but still it is enough

That with these ages come ones like Olive, firm and fragile.

-HSK

Another Poem About Spring

Silken, my

own thoughts from

some happy Greece I one day

bared from bosom to navel

and back down to

my toe-gems, to a wind that massaged

and billowed around

me, in such rounds

of

        playfully

taking up temporary refuge in my hair

(and quite soon would swish back out again) that

My grecian urn scattered

honey *every*where

-LH

A Ratatouille of Divine Love

This doesn't happen often anymore,

Where everything is fresh and whole,

And she cuts into its fragrant firmness;

Usually she buys it pre-cut,

Slightly limp and kind of flavorless,

And dumps it out from clamshells,

Glugs some oil in and calls it stew.

But this time, rain spattering and fronds blustering

Against the window (She saw them move, first,

In the tiny copy of the window

Inside the table of her little gemstone

When she lifted her hand to wipe out sleep,

And she knew her day was unexpectedly,

Gloriously empty)-

This time she chopped/sautéed and chopped/sautéed,

Breath slow, head cocked, movements spare,

And now everything is simmering down to silky thickness,

And peace has spread out from the knot of reminiscence

That was squeezing in her belly

And filled the house with silence

Mingled with eggplant, peppers, thyme, and time.

All will be well, he said, but sometimes

The ages merge for a few hours,

And a circle forms in which

All is well

Right now.

-HSK

Apologies to My Husband

I had it all down just a minute ago
        but it flew off on some dragon's wing.
I go to no effort to do my pain justice,
        just leave my life's blood here to sing;
and I don't know what for and I've nowhere to go,
        and my conscience whips, biting with sting.

I listened to no one, I went on my own,
        determined my own was the best.
It was, and I've always handled the hurt,
        but now all I want is some rest.
It was, but it's building too high and too fast
        and I want to return to the nest.

From razor blades, high places, low minds, and tears,
        from running and hiding and screams,
My savior gently plucked me to hold me forever
        in dappled sundroplets of beams.
He garnished me now with daisies and dizzies
        and softly he polished my dreams.

And I - - I tarnished him, too many times,
        brought him up and then let him fall,
Without meaning to. I simply wanted to help
        but I answered the wrong desperate call;
And now I don't want to see any more
        wild sapphires scattered at all.

-LH

Before the Hysterectomy

this belly

of despair

is my decision:

    Do I die because

           I cannot let go

    Or do I kill off what would

           kill me?

If I fail this lesson

I doom us all

I will create my own hurricane

I am

the eye

and the heart

and the heat,

the chaos

and the stillness of death

the ultimate irony of

guilt and

agony

Surrender has only ever meant pain

Finally I have a grip,

an iron grip

This is control

and if I control

there can be

no surprises

       You will not take any more pieces of me

       I have them tightly wrapped up

And I

and only I

can do them harm now

and I am losing my grip

       This is not fair

The choice is mine

I fear only

that my will is dying, too

-LH

Dominic's Candle

I stood and made a promise by the candle's light-

Lightly (from a sudden need to make a reason),

Reasoning he could not lightly withdraw like that,

That note and gun, his fear of absence-brought-to-light,

Lighting up and fading out without a purpose.

Purposing to fill said light promise (I made one;

One keeps one's promise to the dead, if anything),

Things I thought and should have said before follow here:

Here I am because the thing that eschewed the pills-

Pills bought alone so no one would suspect a thing,

Things being what they were- was a faint micro-hope

Hoping, "I might miss something good." And, Lord, that voice

Voiced truth. Events it chills to know I'd miss include

(Including ones he missed): Voices of our cousins-

Cousins always kids for him- joining ours to voice

Voiceless people's needs, as they grew and found the drive.

Driving, windows down to smell the jasmine. Lights

Lighting wintertime; nights with popcorn and a book.

Booking tickets home, the lights against the snowy

Snow-plowed airport; the reckless joy of our headlights

Lighting up the highway home. Above all others,

(Other lights, internal), light dawning (full delight),

Light kindling a flame in a fatigued mind's grim night:

"For my yoke is easy and my burden is light."

-HSK

18

Correspondence Today

Corrugated boxes	dusted
See	layer upon
Layer these	months
And years churning	gently
In our vastness,	that is to say
The passage of,	the sticky-soft
Clicking of,	enormous dusky
Space I mean	the time
Between	what our individual
Inks, multicolored	and
Calligraphic	poured out
In ongoing pulses	each
Our very	brooks of essence
I have found here	tonight old poetry
And correspondence	that which
Once was part of	my mind
Shifting downward	has become
Synonymous	with my breathing
All that has made us joyous	causes us pain
Our prides and sweets have	separated
Us	you from me
Us from	all that ran
Our brooks	before

I shrink from the   possibility that

All that was my mind   and then

My core   and then

My breath will   continue to shift

Ever lower   and all that I will be

Will be   reduced

-LH

Fern

There was one more thing I wanted to say to you
but I paused to consider my affection
and the line went dead

In that brief moment while I weighed my priorities
came the impact with the cement
the inhale and suspend as you flew to their desperate attempts
the exhale and hold with your head wide open
your blue eyes shut
and you never drew your own breath again

A moment of my rewound memory
caught
and held with my heart wide open
my veins cut open
your fingers shut around my wrist
as you turned around in the car's front seat
and ignored the blood
locked your blue eyes onto my brown
and told me: I was going to be okay now

In all that followed
you never gave up on me,
your faith wide open
Your eyes stayed locked on mine
until you knew it was safe
to continue on your way
to your own sandy-beach fulfillment
never shutting the door on our cosmic dance

You were uplifting and forward

gentle and open

your wisdom so practical

it almost made me laugh out loud,

except that

we were so intertwined that I always knew

before I looked

that you had sent me a message:

"There's a disturbance in the force. What's up?"

So I shut down those who didn't understand you.

We had it, you and I.

You always looked up

and so I

looked up the next morning and saw your message

—   bears this time -

and this time

I laughed out loud,

my mouth wide open, my eyes wide open, my love wide open

and shut out the ridiculous idea that

you were gone

Our friendship lives on

Open and shut.

-LH

Patter

A preacher
Spoke on video
Poorly cut
Practical
Behind her, house keys jingled
And set off a rush

That started
With a cold brooklet
Running on
Slick pebbles
Through a garden of capiz
And bamboo wind chimes

Stirring in
The coruscations
Of autumn
Sun showers
Under aspen leaves clapping
In sunny homage

And advanced
Beyond a figure
Pouring out
Blueberries
Into a blue-glazed soup bowl
With a dim patter

In passing
Stirring his faded
Skirt into
Gauze ripples
And pushing open the door
To rustle pages

In the books
Then swirling next door
To murmur
With shoppers
Over herbs and vinegar
Through the dry bright air

In the crowd's
Soft susurration
Swelling to
A roar with
Tires crunching on gravel
Into a clearing

In the pines.
Here is harmony
Beneath stings
And grasping:
The echoes of a spirit
Hovering above

Dark waters.

-HSK

Desire

He asked me what I wanted
and I said, "I want nothing."

I want to know, irrevocably and unquestionably,
that everything is alright,
and I want nothing.

I want to feel the roots of your arms around me
and the rock of your chest behind me
even when I am not with you
but especially when I am with you
I want to feel you
I want to feel you
I want to feel you

I want my missteps to be backed up
by the solidity of your footprints,
every turn I take
certain or uncertain
to be held and moved forward, redirected and guided along
I want yes
and yes and yes and yes
and I want nothing
When I shake I want you to hold the space around me,
containing my electricity in the shelter of your allowance
I want you to allow me the space you've always allowed me
and I want you to be there in it with me

I want you to pin me to the earth,

the vise of your hands like a guarantee,

and make me hear you whisper that you are here,

that you want me

When I search I want to feel substance

I want my hands to sink into something and wrap around it,

not to come up entangled only in themselves

I want you to build pillars under my words

when I don't even understand my own voice

I want to be able to sit in silence with you for hours

I want us to look into each others' eyes and remember

I want you to adore me

out loud and loudly

giving voice and movement to the roundness of your laughing passion,

until it reverberates off of the overturned bowl of the sky

and I want you to do it day in and day out

I want the thought to be taken care of

before it is even formed

What I ask for is as intangible and impermanent as spun sugar

that disintegrates on my tongue,

And so I reply to him, "I want nothing."

-LH

Prairie Hymn

On high prairie in the Sunday void

Of an unthinkably vast sky,

It's easy grace to subside

Until the thunderheads

And brittle grasses

Are sufficient

To be my

Bread and

Hymn.

-HSK

Hash Brown Elegy

What is clear is that, tonight,
As I was sniffling over the second batch of onions,
No apparition drifted into the kitchen
That was thick with butter
To lend its meaning to the blindness
Of leaking eyes and liquid sinuses.

Last night, I knelt beside the holy whiteness
Of porcelain and water
And stayed, keening for the buddies
Of a broken soldier whose face I never learned.
It was easier to comprehend their silences;
It makes more sense, tonight,
To purse my lips at too much pepper.

-HSK

Dominic

This is not just about what you have done.

And what you have done is opened up a
Pandora's box of such hurt
that I cannot feel past my memories.
They are swamping me
snaking their tendrils around my chest and
pulling me down into the swamps
of my alligator-infested youth in the south.
Going south,
I am raw,
the skin flayed from my body leaving me exposed,
every nerve exposed,
every beat of my heart
more painful than the last.
You did this.
You bastard,
I know you didn't do this.
Please, God, tell me he didn't do this.

This is the stuff of nightmares.
The violent shaking of my head
cannot dislodge the vision
I cannot stop seeing.
Were you sitting cross-legged on your bed?
Did your cat see?
What was the last thought that brain had?
Did you remember our conversation of the day before?
Had I helped in any way?
Did I give you the idea?

This is not just about what you have done.

And what you have done is paused our lives mid-stride,

halted the air on its way to our lungs,

froze the blood, deep,

on its path to our own life-giving organs,

so that a part of each of us died with you.

Unable to bear the horror -

What have you done?! -

I turned off my light so I wouldn't have to see anymore.

And I have forgotten how to turn it back on.

You did this.

How could you do this to us?

Please, God, help me undo this.

This is not just about what you have done.

And what you have done

is perverted your own name,

now leaden in our bellies,

caught unuttered on our tongues,

the breath yanked from our love if we dare

to breathe life into it,

into your name.

We are afraid we will crumble if we say it out loud

and so

alone in our cars,

quiet in our beds,

we whisper it with experimental terror

and we scream it

to curse you

to bring you back

to beg for a rewind

of all of our failings.
How did we fail you?
Where did we fail you?
We cannot bear to know that we failed you
so we swallow your name again,
Dominic.

This is not just about what you have done.

And what you have done
is undone all the work my little-girl self
put into protecting your mother from pain as we grew up.
I cannot fight a ghost
and so again, I curse you, I skirt your name.
So much easier to rage at your nothingness
than to remember your sunshine.
Oh, you were sunshine.
A swing and a miss.
I miss you.

This is not just about what you have done.

And what you have done
is cracked us open
so we can see
all the smooth, clean pieces inside
untarnished because
we have never touched them
our glances don't rest there
and barely acknowledge
as they slide carefully to the safe shallows.
You have forced us to poke
to mar the perfection

to overturn

to expose the dark, damp roots to daylight.

This is about what you have done.

And what you have done

is helped us turn to each other

and ask the questions

and listen.

We asked each other

Have you hurt, too?

And suddenly we were not alone.

Suddenly we could say anything.

Suddenly you were gone.

And you gave us each other.

-LH

Inarticulate

Help me speak for you on this afternoon of relentless heat and stillness,

Let me call up the peculiar choking scent of baking dust

And then rise up above it in terpenic stainless air

To survey hot rips of highway in the sagebrush

And the sweaty tramp of daily walkers,

Let my swollen fingers spread out,

My voice roll like thunder

To shower down

Sweet ease.

-HSK

The Day Before the Razor Blade

I no longer know my beginning

my end

nor the tangle of spirals that

comprise my now

oscillating

ebbing and flowing

it has flung me back down to the absolute

I can't be here again

I've done this already

I don't understand myself in time and space

Nothing is certain but the red jab of uncertainty

and it has consumed me

swallowed me -

not whole but shredded

into unrecognizable bits

unfathomable depths

The face in the mirror is

Picasso-like

piecemeal and distorted

I don't recognize myself,

the plane of my cheek

the pain of my soul dying

"You have been here before," it whispers.

"You know what to do."

Ah, but I also know how to wield

a sharp shard of glass

I walk past it, hands clenched

only because I promised someone that I would

(I can't remember who. I wish it were me.)

This is killing me.

Breath fails me
I pull hard at the air
heart pounding
but I can't bring enough in
My chest hurts
I want to stop hurting

So help me God, I can't remember how

And then after I stop hurting
I want to celebrate
Let me move to rhythms I
know in the universe
Let me sing my joy
that I once knew,
my complete satisfaction
swirling out like multicolored ribbons
as I twirl, as I embrace as I laugh my gratitude
Only don't make me do it alone

Let me move side-by-side with you
so the welling in my chest can ease
Let me finish this out with you
Help me remember
how you love me
Make me believe
that you love me
Help me. Please help me.

I can't feel you anymore
and your own Picasso face frightens me
Where have you gone?

I have never been more lonely

I am

wailing with the red jab of uncertainty

dying with the red-stained jagged edges

of glass shards

screaming – and not at you -

"What do you want from me?!"

Quietly, suddenly, completely

I have run out of things to say

I am done talking,

crying, prodding, pleading, explaining, questioning

Nothing left to share

It's your turn

I stand quietly

in my red and black agony

Waiting

-LH

The Likeness

The leaders, led, and lost make vague, wavering forms

In the humid night to ask, for the love of God,

To be loved as they were made for love, and not robbed

Of the good gifts made for dealing out equally:

Time, and the right to deserve one's reputation.

The night flickers like the shadow of their servant,

A blurred phantom of the flawless love whose likeness

Stamps the half-hidden faces of the nervous men

And women, moving in an unsettled fashion

Through the wet summer scent of mown lawn, not humbled

By the starry, shifting blaze of cars, or the deaths

That brought them here, the mass of loss so vast it crossed

Harsh-lit highways to gather people exalted

By their passion, to call out in mourning the names

That permeate the park. On dew-soaked, itchy knees,

The fluid shadows count the seconds (shoulders bowed

With the heaviness of a thousand hurtful things)

Under the weird glare of clouded city heavens.

In time, the strangers rise to stretch and shake off earth

That clings and smells of damp. In love they've given tongue

To pain and fear, to demand that we confess

We share the cast of God. Cries of "Hell" and "Jesus"

Lace the dark, abbreviated prayers to the Lord

To make us spare the next brother, son, or father.

-HSK

Makeshift Office

A padded

Mat and rough-woven

Throw wait for

Afternoons

When he can drop in weary

Gratitude to sleep

-HSK

Frustration in Full

what

do I want to don't
you see it's

all slipping a

lone, here
I aren't someone... someone...
I can't
remember; I don't
know why now,
can't get by, how
can I ever tell my darling
what even I don't know

-LH

Fern, Refashioned

Abruptly she was lost, yes, and:

Vibrance lost left howling waste, but:

Those ashes in a savior's hand

Form ashen feathers; this is what,

Destroyed, rebuilt, forms love from dust

To build his city- so we trust

That mercy doesn't lightly lie

In stowing souls we love nearby,

Secured from heavy suffering.

It often seems a starker thing.

-HSK

Gratitude

Sometimes the most that can be asked of you
is that you close your eyes in gratitude
that you are still standing

Do that, and it won't matter
that bits of you seem to be dangling
at odd angles
At least they are still there
and you will find that that is enough

Close your eyes and breathe
It is All. Right. Now.

If the world you inhabit shifts
so that its smooth, secure knowledge
fractures into mirror pieces,
be still
Remember that you are at the center of it all
and have only to Be as it revolves,
and that also you are completely insignificant
Be grateful that you don't matter

Have gratitude that none of this
is about you
There is a beautiful freedom within
If the touch of the night on your
morning-glory self
curls your blossom inward,
have faith that the light will come again,
and in gratitude open yourself to the possibility
You will blossom again
You are still standing

-LH

Staying Power

Deep in the din of sin
I'm deafened by its roar
The hardest choice is staying
But You told me, "Stay"
You showed me

Your

Self

Littering the
Glittering the land

Your hand that scatters hope
And there is no better way
I want no other home

I:
Embrace the blight
Take up my cross

-HSK

In the Courthouse
(The Murder of Hope)

The ghastly point

you harpooned into me -

into my core

into my womb

       Home

to the origins of

triple suicides

Death by loving

and desertation

and withholding all I

hold precious and vital

You forced me to find

new vitality,

new reasons,

new things to love

Having stolen from me my three points

of life

Made me learn to love

what I could not

You killed me in triplicate

That ghastly point

you harpooned into me

was not sharp and singular,

though the pain was vivid,

it struck and erupted

like those exploding bulletheads

shattering every part of me

the poison spreading to where I didn't even

know I could feel any longer...

You are a vicious mongrel with excellent aim

and I loved you once

-LH

Aftermath

There's never much of anything left after these long evenings,

But wrapping it up for tomorrow seems right, anyway.

I guess it's some musty memory of empty fridges.

Plus, I'd like to retire, and those leftovers really add up over a lifetime.

-HSK

Memorable Music

Always within
the Japanese paper,
the linen, the foxtail where
two of us sat,
is where the disaster
of heavy-downed
music
and wails in the music
come back here
to rat

on me,
and my eyes burn,
my lashes
pool back all
the drum solos beating the bed
where, for too
many centuries, I watered the pillow,
which grew, and it cushioned my head.

It's science, I said,
just the chemistry of how
we all run, and anyhow
I'm trying;
but that music is
from the beginning
of Glorious Times -
so why am I crying?

-LH

Mr. A. and Beth

He wasn't even that old, just kind of tired

Waiting on a ratty ottoman in the arcade,

Its flaked gilt shrouded by the popcorn-scented murk,

His shoulders hunched at the midday ghosts of beeps and clacks

From years of frenzied games. He spoke uninvited,

As people do, mumbling at the nervous employee

About a loveless, callous, braggadocious age,

About lives plundered for lush gardens, aliens bound.

The worker shifted her gaze to the scuffed consoles

And pretended not to hear. He groaned to a bent stand

As his long love approached, then pronounced distinctly,

"But they always killed the prophets," and took an elbow.

The glass door flashed fire as they entered into

The blazing oven of the summer day. Behind them,

The central air kicked to life with a rushing roar.

-HSK

Warm Water

She joins my shower to take refuge from the threats
She finds in Sunday fellowship, a body more
Aligned with where my head is. Slowly, now the wet

Air, stirred by entry, swirls like wings unfurling; for
Relief we hum our song, but in an aching while
It's hard to know if we are harmonizing or

Are keening faintly under lost and grieving smiles
Above the angel choir of shower droplets
Soft ringing sweetly on the soap-slick tiles.
That song abides, no matter if we're reconciled.

-HSK

Last/First

But ask first, will it last-
The estate you've amassed
It's reversed at the last
When the chain of the past
Will be cast off those cursed
By the grip of the first-
In their lack; they'll slake thirst
And at last, they'll be first.

-HSK

Helpless Bystander

It was a smudged-up piece of charcoal
with a million blood-stained eyes,
and in writhing desperation
my lilied hands
groped like the blind around it,
but the silence of duty stretched onward for eternities
so my hands of fear
wrung each other alone.

It was a mirror of deception
in a hideous, distorted circus
where with confusion and cries uttered in lumps
my image wavered and sneered,
and behind it was the only peaceful spot of all.

It was a stone-tipped spear
and a red-tipped spear
grinding stone against bone of abstraction,
and a rose, and a rusted spring,
and mulberry splinters deep within flesh,
and screams and distress,
and distressed laughter in churches.

It was my horror upon realizing
the plunge being taken into ethereal depths
of metal,
and my useless shrieking
and my trodding delicately with cries of anguish

-LH

Inspiration/Expiration

In a thing as small as expired cream,
Which says, "set me aside, rise up, forget,"
Even there the spirit lit a new light
And then decamped when it was time to go.
Aware or not, we move from place to place,
Leaping from one rock to the next hard place:
Where the spirit moves, there we jump to go.
We leave the dark for the pool of lamplight
When it shifts. We fear because we forget:
By nature we discard expired cream.

We follow light. We'll find that better place.

-HSK

On Breathing

It was with crystalline eyes that
I viewed porcelain Freedom

emerging
from

such surrealistic walls as
only known to a self-murderer;

and fluidity?
Oh, gracefully laced with this-is!
This is the peace

for which you whimpered,

this is
the honesty you begged for from your solitude
Clear and pure,
with heart-wrenching "yes"es
Madonna! I cried, but she left me hanging.

-LH

Dusk on the Patio

Yesterday the cardinals sang good night,
Not worrying about the coming dark
Or the storm approaching,
Certain that one of two things would happen:
One: day would be so good
As to come again.
Two: the night would close in
Gently.

I thought, maybe my nest is too feathered;
I'm uneasy about the coming dark.
In the storm approaching,
There used to be a sort of recklessness:
Poor: as long as day came,
I had everything.
Naked: night was always
Welcome.

-HSK

On the Verge

Sweetness
wrings me, wrecks me
crescendoes, upsets me.

This is forbidden,

yet I cannot keep hidden
the sense of familiarity and home
of recognition
and submission
I knew you once before -

It was centuries ago in Eden
ever sweetened
by "No"
and we know
we cannot do this.

We must not do this.

Back away from me

Stop watching

Stop touching

Stop imploring

Stop your gypsy eyes from boring

into mine, into me,

making me finally, fully see

If I let myself, I'd fall,

feathers, leaden-weight, and all

so utterly completely

wrenching, horribly, so sweetly

into the most devastating honesty

and clarity ever known -

into your perfect abyss.

This

is ethereal and tangible

and achingly unmanageable.

We cannot do this.

-LH

Crude

You'll have to excuse me for what I have:

This crudely formed Christianity

Like a granite boulder roughly carved

Into the vague likeness of a man.

When your heart smiles at known trees as friends

And congratulates the old bricks on their beauty,

It's hard to shake the guilty notion

That friendship has suffused the world's substance.

When books were husks of words that whispered nothing,

And the world spoke to me instead on your behalf,

I've had to shrug and take the things the world said

And, for the rest, to rest in nescient faith.

If, in soul if not in fact, I've worshipped you

In sunny groves, for glory in their greenness,

If I've set you up in that bright space inside

Too much like a standing stone among the ferns,

Then by your grace I've claimed, make up the lack

And turn the stone into the perfect man.

I heard you in the forest first, so now

Call me along; talk me beyond it.

-HSK

One

I hold in my hands
the heart of God

and I understand why
this very essence
of the very essence
is perfectly still,
why it does not
throb with the pulse
of life and love,
beating a steady cadence
to draw all into it

all is one already

I know why
it is so still it seems
inanimate,
its purple-white radiance
just
being
laying there
contentedly
nestled in my palms

My fingers that curl
up to cradle it
cannot feel it
but know it is there
It just
is

And I understand
but cannot tell you
I don't
know how

I hold in my hands
the heart of God
who laid it there
in absolute faith

-LH

Veiled

The world has gone gray and sort of misty,

I'm not sure why. Thought I had it figured out.

I'm waiting for the hurricane to blow in.

It's got to be there somewhere, off the shoreline.

The pool of light has dwindled to a thread now,

So ridiculously thin that if I look,

Not sideways, but directly, it just might snap.

Thank God, I was given miracles to hold.

If my active faith is giving out too fast,

Their memory is faith, as much as any.

Fragile though they are, they'll pull me through the gloom

To the cloudless edge, where I still wait on God.

-HSK

Hurricane

After another private hurricane
Inside our cramped and dog-smelling sedan
We sat stunned in messy traffic, staring-
Staring bleakly at the inner wasteland
With uniform gray flatness passing by
As if the storm inside broke out and lay
Waste to the peninsula.

And there I was, defenselessly sitting
In a still small silence, and finally
After that, not wondering where You are.
Somewhere in the driving bewilderment
Of rain, I shifted to the right and found:
Myself, inside the temperate world
Of faith in absent goodness.

That's one small half a universe closer
To my kindly silent God.

-HSK

Serenity

When did you become so small?
It used to be
you were so huge you filled
my entire vision
your presence, all-encompassing,
comprised my world
There was a time
when your energy forced its way into
every dim corner of my mind
and every thump of my overworked heart
I could think of
and feel
and see
no other

I wonder were you aware of,
as I was,
the vein that throbbed right in the middle
of your expansive forehead
when you had me
with my back against the wall,
screaming obscenities
and detailing my ideal death
?
You would say:
I didn't lay a hand on you that time
But that vein
and the decibel of your rage
sent me
loose-kneed
down the wall

and into merciful oblivion

as surely as if you'd pushed me

You were huge

when you followed me

at a distance all over town

and paid others to do the same

Do you remember

how I whirled

when I heard the click of the camera

in the bushes,

how my pupils contracted in the

POP! of the flash, growing smaller with the rest of me?

I know you know

You were there

even if you weren't there

I can sing for you the song

of how it felt

when you shook my very foundation

Every word

every thought

every whisper

every cry

every prayer

every pulse of my goddamned heart

became

Let Me Go

      let me go

or one of us will kill me

I missed the exact moment

when you no longer occupied me

I must have been too busy living

When I open my door and

you are standing there

you are

so very minute

I have cleaned you from the dimmest reaches

and I have

rewound the film in that camera

I am sad for you

knowing

that you will always stay tucked up inside it,

wound as tightly as a spring,

afraid that if you are exposed to light

you will leave no impression

I was elsewhere you began to lose your bulk

Peace to you.

-LH

Toffee

She reaches for warm toffee
But fingers bump glass
And tingle from frost
Strange how the hairline
Crack heals and hides
With every tap of chilled
Knuckles/blue palms
And the toffee winks
Indifferently

-HSK

Seascape

I keep circling back to those white sand dreams

(Or is it snow) and the biting zircon waves

That cause absolute elation

And absolute dread

To bleed and run together even though

They wash harmlessly around me

And the whales are the most terrifying

Gorgeous things

Spinning

And who knows what else is with me in their sphere?

Is heaven in not just the triumph but

The

Terror,

Too?

I never felt a cleaner fear than this

That chastens

And

Exalts.

When you roll over and wake up instead of

Drowning

In the

Whirl

Where do you go from there?

What does the splashing icy green-blue globe

Have to do with:

A dry breakfast

And then:

A traffic jam?

It takes hours at the office to warm

Away the deep sea chill inside my belly,

Layers of the daily grime to darken

The dazzle coming off its crystal swells.

Why do we go from there

Where heaven nearly ringed us?

For now, we do the dirty work assigned

And treasure in us memories of fear.

I think it must be:

That we leave the seascape for the mire

Is sweet heaven's

Saddest

Sorrow,

Purest

Praise.

-HSK

The Cycle

There are times,

he mumbled around the tattered

dry cigar, when the bus comes ramblin' on my

way and I realize

(spitting a stream of something putrid

between his lips

and watching it splatter on the pavement)

that afterall what it's

doing is just

takin' me round back to

where I just

gotta get up and do it all over again,

and he rearranged his stiffened eyebrows

and hitched up his pants

to sigh onto the dirty white bench

behind him

-LH

Moving Back to Colorado

There are tears in my heart
       (I'm coming home, I'm
       coming home)
Pain as beautiful as what rolls gently past
my window,
what rises directly in front of me,
taking my breath
to breathe a life into these mountains
The aspens are brilliant yellow,
fiery orange,
and stacked
layer upon endless layer
defining harmony with the evergreens

Baby rivulet of rivers
       (I'll be home soon, I'll
       be home)
I see crispness
I see rocks
along the bottom
through the clear
they give the river
her song

I hand you this
It is free
It is all that's meant to be

I am home,
I've come home,
I am speechless.
Beauty hurts.

-LH

Self-Inflicted Homesickness

Perversely
Turning down the road
That's leading
All the way
Across the continent from
The home of longing-

So far that
Probably never
Will it be
Actual
Home, a granite-crisp refuge
From a bitter earth.

So instead
It retreats from the
Dream surface,
Tucks itself
Into the place where longing
Becomes a playhouse.

Then it's years
Before a new home
Forms itself
In the heart
Of a little white wood church
With a tidy lawn.

-HSK

He's Perfect, Thanks

This little wigglebutt's pugnacious.
Attempts at love he finds vexatious;
Stay on your side of the bed, or get the boot.

Oh, and by the way, his audacious
Claims of starving are fallacious-
I just fed him; his hunger's not acute-

In spite of which, he is tenacious
In his begging and voracious
With your food, though not his, the picky brute.

He flirts with strangers, though ungracious
To his humans; he's disputatious
When it comes to baths (and resolute).

In guarding toys, he's pertinacious,
If, regarding ownership, mendacious-
Contentious in all things. Thank God he's cute.

-HSK

Un/Shaken

these people who felt a loss and loss and then a loss;
i want to pray for their keeping and to know.

what i want to say is that -
but what i want to say is beneath words
is just the native bleat of indignation
accusing you of not keeping them safe and warm and fed enough
so what i want to say fades away into
forlorn mumbling and then to silent sitting
aghast at all this ghastliness
bleeding from its awful beauty
i want to loathe myself for noticing its beauty,
would rather pity without other stirring

and what i want to say is that

i want to say

i want

hold this

-HSK

Ingathering

Here they are, the waterborne, blood-begot,

Swaying slightly on the clement lake

Of Your care, Your cordial watching,

In Your crystal light like no other morning.

This is where Your blood has brought them

In its hyaline outflowing course-

And if its whorls felt like a riptide

On the way, low visibility

Will make the senses sharp like that.

But here they are now, mists dispersed, selves gathered

Richly, perfectly together

In the glass-golden, aqua-purled,

Clearest morning ever known. They are here,

Your honor. And am I one? Am I one?

-HSK

Frances

This is how we mourn her:

With gentle equilibrium in the knowing

That she left her brightest selves with us.

Still there in the shifting shade like water patterns

In the dust-dry summer air,

Like penciled dappled blossoms on her watercolor paper,

Like the balm of silver Russian olive in the baking heat.

This is how we mourn her:

With soft sorrow like a shimmered thread that runs through

Every lovely loving hour.

Still there in the fractured frost-glow of our candles

On the winter windowsill,

In the trouble-crinkled eyes that enrich the rosy laughter,

In the golden time of silence right before the ancient prayer.

This is how we mourn her:

Always, and with wonder.

-HSK

A Very Long Wait

I was amazed that it took me so long
To recognize you and your mighty hand.
In the slick-floored kitchen,
You smiled at me in my giddy spinning.
I thought you were a ghost.
I smiled, too, and left.
Half a life ago, just-
Walked out.

Even though you filled that night with sun,
By the blaze of you with your mighty hand
In the slick-floored kitchen-
I dismissed you as a ghost; and later,
When angels sang to me
Of bitterness, then
Inexpressible joy,
I thought:

Nothing at all. What a nice dream, I said.
And not until you, with your mighty hand
From the slick-floored kitchen,
The angels' song, my bitterness, then joy-
Created a life's psalm
Of pain and beauty
Did I recognize the
Bridegroom.

I've come to find out it's like that sometimes.

If I had recognized your mighty hand

In the slick-floored kitchen,

It might have been a lazy sort of faith.

As with the disciples

With whom you broke bread,

There was reason for the

Waiting.

-HSK

Illness, Ingrate

I still resent
Being slow/tired
This puzzling decay

It's maybe meant
Being weak/thwarted
To place worth

On pure being
Being bent/sullen
I defy it

-HSK

The Body That Was Broken For Us

See: face's fixed lines, faintly indicative
Of fretfulness; sighing limp, lugubrious:
A lifetime's toil tapered down to plaintive
Aching, bound in senescent retrospect, thus
Base, bored to breaking, broadened and embittered
But never breaking faith with the binding word
Crucified, confirmed in blood, in foolishness:
Cleansed, clarified someday to an endless "yes!"

See: hangdog harried reticence, slackened post-
Hounding, having found late a home of ruthful
Civil indifference to early crimes the ghosts
Of which still raid the Christ-craving mind, rueful
Not knowing what led to where how, but later
Less abashed, clear through the world-blinded blur
Will perceive in plainness how it went that way-
The why of all, goodwill of all, on that day.

See: theatrical by training and by trait
The polished pretty that draws side-eyed distrust
Charged with fraud through native need to moderate
More limelight tones, deny the stage-side stardust
Way of speech. Tighter draws the greasepaint pulling
Of misjudged isolation, louder flinging
Lines for anyone. The thrashing then will cease,
Mad trilling theater stilled in collective peace.

See: Seeing all but self-salvation, certain
Sinful squalor is the sum of self, softened
In reprieve of others, their gentle human
Faultiness, fragile sweetness, freed in the end
Through being children- but self is no child
Chilled, choked by thorns, chosen by the sweet mild
Lamb, but how, how to hold on to amnesty?-
Will love the self as a limb of deity.

So: closely bound, the limbs of Christ, pre-broken
Broken every branch, limping aching - boundless
Then though bound now to spoil boasting, spoken
For already out of love. Look, see soundness
In the broken body's future, highest king,
The loveliness surpassing understanding:
Glad lowness for the sweet leading, magnified
To heal, then to show: all are justified.

-HSK

Rush Hour

Windshield
Diamonds glisten
Swaying down the highway
West in grimy traffic blazing
Post-rain.

-HSK

Gardenia

So then you slow down for a little stretch, and

One pale gardenia starts to open

Inside the cavity

Of aching in your tired chest, so now

For a heartbeat or two

You've heard Him speaking;

You'll keep that bloom till it

Ignites.

-HSK

The Late Snow

In May
Up north the pines
Can fill with snow like grains
Of silver sand that smell like home
And rest.

-HSK

Thought for a Mountain Lake

May have been intended, that

emerald-toned mirror

through which the aquamarine undersea

is,

as here,

> Precious Adequacy

> Alongside and Hushed

refreshing an imagery undisturbed

above its napping Morpheus

-LH

The Wild City

This day is gray and windy like the cities of
littoral holidays and bitter, bitter cold.
here's the weird white-feathered ice with simple daylight
showing through, cleaner than isopropyl and far
stiller. And here's the chocolate taste at the back of
the throat, the savor of happy expectancy,
a cold air flavor with a future added in;
what future, though? Linked I think to faint voices in
the mock metro air, ice shine brighter than it should
be for the cloud cover, rare buoyancy in a
body that is weighing down too soon, the better
class of reminiscences built on a homely
fellowship. Too much world, is what it is; days
like this one, some of it lifts away to leave a
thinner silence, through which a different city can
be heard. A wait-a-while city, a city
like a city you could love, a city with a
day-glow at its wild center, where the feathers
are not locked in ungiving ice, but fall freely.

-HSK

My Companion

There's a miserable little demon
who sits upon my shelf
- Instead of eyes, has rolling fog
- the dampness of his health
attributed to loneliness, boredom, fear, fatigue.
The demon's name is Self.

He has so very, very much
he thinks he has to say,
and when he speaks his ears turn down;
they fold and hide away.
And in the end he speaks no good:
I kill him every day -

Yet there he sits, still,
his back against the gold-bright gong
of early mornings, early evenings
and it echoes yet, "You're wrong",
and I wonder why the process by which
we're dying, dying, dying
has to take so very long?

It's true I exhaust more muscles when I frown

than when he grins back.

What a paradox! I

mirrored back: doubled!

Leapt! then,

troubled, slept, but I do not know

why I sit there so still

in make-up as a mime,

and I *cannot* understand

why it takes so long a time....

-LH

The One You Win by Losing

Look, this film set flimsiness failed to fulfill;

Here's a human's will's work, not any work of His.

The trick's to look beyond and will His wider will-

No easy trick; instead, a daunting tough campaign

Won by seizing ruins at the top of every hill:

Every hill of self-willed effort a lost travail

Repeated and repeated to exhaustion till

In urgency surrender comes (and may with fury),

That release enabling rest inside His wiser will

Which washes souls headlong into entire work, that is

That which, to total fullness, will leave each life fulfilled.

-HSK

Two Surgeons

Her figure, dressed in white to reassure
(And funny, now, to still desire that)
Went pixelated into a Monet
His over-lushly growing garden ponds:
The coat and face bits efflorescing to
Abundant waving blooms around a ground
Of algae green (the awful clinic walls).
A garden's better than the room, at least.
The call, however, ended and there was
A higher ratio than there was before
Of mysteries to answers to explore.
The pathways multiply like fractals, such
That time will finish first, before each path
Can be explored to bring the ratio down
To one. That's when the answer, singular,
Was given, and it was the one that came
In vlogs, in shows, in essays all last month:
Slow down. Slow down. Slow down, or be slowed down.
The gift that came in triplicate: the Son,
The Father, Holy Ghost, revealed again
In one more glory, multiplied by three.
The garden for the soothing, mystery
To give surrender, and the answer for
The triumph: stop, then listen, then relate.
It's wild: triple blessings, evermore.

-HSK

Christopher

For awhile your name held nothing but pain,

screamed out in the shower stall,

reverberated loud and hollow in the car

We shouted it, cried it,

moaned it, begged

for answers through

the moniker of all that you were

and all that you could have been

and it came to me from a place not frightened

but free

The gentle wooden notes of a flute

caressed me into an understanding without words,

an answer without speaking,

slid gently under my why's and wisely

patted you down to your origins

and smoothed me out as well

I know now it's okay to know

I will always miss you

You have been silently sung away

to the place where you're no longer frightened

You're free

-LH

Not Quite Eden, But Still

Everything that breathes will praise His name.
Even in these pots against the wall,
Sprouting green called praises as it came.

Plastic pot pews ring as they proclaim
Liberty from darkness: call by call,
Everything that breathes will praise His name.

Heaven's hearts, we can't not do the same-
Leap (in heart) and praise in song- when all
Sprouting green called praises as it came.

Glory be to gardens! They inflame
Cravings for the king of song; recall:
Everything that breathes will praise His name.

Eden turned to this and shows our shame;
But, to One who took our fitting fall,
Sprouting green called praises as it came.

Little wonder, when kind Christ became
Our Lamb: even in a yard this small,
Everything that breathes will praise His name;
Sprouting green called praises as it came.

-HSK

Firstfruits

This first month,
It's one small
Tomato

Tinier
Than my chipped
Thumbnail

But, oh man,
That taste is
So intense.

-HSK

A Heady Year

Today, as every day:

Honey amber gates swing open

Serving access to a heady orchard's

Apples picked, dipped, and eaten

For sweetening the lips and tongue

To make a year of honey gentle words:

Beginning words become, so

Mouths need honeying the most

For somewhere keeping souls in concord

When life's lemon panes crash in candy shatters

Scattering shards, sugar sparkling. Eat the honey.

Eat it anyway; read it all the same.

Sweeten life in doubt, among the fragments;

Leap into another year with sticky fingers,

With crystals at the corners of your mouth:

The taste will come; this orchard feeds the nations.

-HSK

Fire Spoke For Us

When we realized we had nothing
To talk about, we lounged, defeated,
Looking into the flames like words
Hurled desperately against the night,
And, at the center, perfect peace.
No wonder fire was thought to be
The digestion of the gods.
It speaks from silence;
It consumes forever.

-HSK

Two-Man Angel Band

Go and pick your way slow over the icy patches on the way home.
Head towards those two men standing under the lamp, and they'll carol
you home.

You'll see how easy it is to leave your own crying self behind you.
Leave her to her grief- or relief- with a new song, and strike out for home.

Go slow, now, though. I know there's an eagerness to get where you're going-
You'll get there in God's good time. They'll wait till you reach them, to sing
you home.

Great-Grandfather Isaac, he's patient. Cousin Isaiah suffers long.
That true lamp's not burning out, and they know the exact tune to get home.

I'll tell you something true: The love of the ages isn't tentative.
It's a cold street in the dark, but they'll carry your tune all the way home.

-HSK

Keeper

Having believed
The light was on forever
I was startled
Felt godforsaken
Fruitless- pruned-
When it burned out.

Then
With no visual reference
No signpost
Pointing the way
To living water
To quench this dying thirst
You spoke
And said just

Wait

And here we are!
We, not I.

You are
My brother bringing freedom
My father granting pardon
My mother bearing treasure
My watcher in the darkness

You Are.

And I
Am not
Afraid.

-HSK

God with the Desperate

I'll tell you the why of it all:
Who looks for God when they're replete?
I was Israel and Judah.
I knew glory after glory-
As in good wine and company
In the years after a savior.
Who needs a refuge in glory?
God is the rock of the failed.

By His mercy, I have failed.
By His grace, I've needed refuge.
By His love, I've needed saving.
By His care, I've been abandoned.
I've been razed and turned to face Him.
As in Israel and Judah,
My kingdom fell to build a need.
Don't tell me God's in His heaven.

God dwells among the desperate,
The King of all those who need Him.

-HSK

Slapdash Neighbors

Next to the next house they have weeds eating their lawn-
Also, the sidewalk is all crunchy with a fall
Mixture of acorns and dead twigs. Who hasn't been drawn
Onto such sidewalks to enjoy that snappy small

Thrill? And they love all the exuberant small lives
Breathing their praise on that small lot! And they do sing
Inner hosannas to the Lord who makes them thrive.
Christmastime, utterly assured- between the clean

Neighbors' yards full of tidy decorations, matched
Smartly- they jumble their collection of diverse
Lights with their lawn ornaments, pleased enough to watch
Lights twinkling randomly, and headlights throwing bursts,

On the long grass, of vibrant color from decor-
Singing, throughout all, hallelujah! There's delight
Coming and now; this little beauty reflects more
Perfectly beautiful abundance, which is light,

Endlessly! Yes! And yes, they thrive, just like their lot:
Slapdash, and stretching for sun, letting it suffice-
Living haphazard and magnificently unfussy lives, but
Oh, their hosannas are exquisitely precise.

-HSK

Retention Pond Jesus

Toward evening I stopped beside
A small retention pond; inside
Its mirror was a wider place
Where scrubby pines stretched out in pride

To mimic cedars' forceful grace;
One straggly maple spread a blaze
Of holy flame; polluted clouds
At sunset turned to silver lace

To serve that Eden as a shroud
To say, "not yet."- but then a crowd
Of twilight insects stirred the gauze.
Right where their ripples met I found

The faintest flicker of a cross-
A victor's token of its loss
When what was on it rose again-
Its crime could not destroy our God.

This weapon of ungentle men
We keep with us in scorn of sin,
Our foe He broke and walked away.
In vain that viciousness. Amen.

The birds began an end-of-day
Devotion song above the gray
Routine of traffic. Heaven waits
In springs for us to join their praise.

-HSK

Before We Met

The way

She came alive

Down south as memories

Arose and washed like waves and sand-

It stung.

-HSK

Peace on Earth, Goodwill to Shoppers

It was time for shopping, late and hurried-
The way that we recall with sheepish grins-
Thirty, sixty, one hundred times concede

It was not as fun as it should have been.
In the crowded parking lot, tire chains
Crunched and groaned absurdly in snow so thin.

And more things were jangling in the crowd's strain:
Forms flicked in and out of the fluorescent
Lights, faces tightened with the grouch of stained,

Wet socks, and of coats they would not relent
To remove in the overheated mall,
Too taxing to pull off in the intent

Evening's rush. Outsized teddy bears sprawled
On grim, configurable shelves in plaid
Or velvet bows; at all ages, we all

Paused to covet the memories we had
Of their narcotic softness, redolent
Of early cinnamon, pajama-clad

Red-and-green mornings under the silent
Fairy lights. Carols (the bastardized ones
That always made us itch for and lament

The beauty they forsook, so when we'd done
Our shopping we would idly search our
Phones for better versions) were set to run

In their worn tracks. In that sweet and sour
Night, too many links were in discordant
Tangles. Under an irked shopper's glower,

I briefly closed my eyes, breathed slow, and bent
My head, and shook it, rattled chains loose, then
Settled them into chiming chords. They blent

Into the soft song of settled age, when
There are storage bins of memory for
Rummaging, and the further song of men

Who saw an everlasting change the more
Gorgeous because it both started the day
We honor in our muddled way, and for

All of us, is still to come when we lay
Aside our burdens. Outside, light flurries
Of snow kept coming, covering in gray-

Salting down this night as a memory
To call up sometime in eternity.

-HSK

Violins

simply
muse the aching notes belonging to a so-seeming
intricate melody,
low belonging to solemn
tearful in the orchestra house

the lone lover upon a stage
strokes his masterpiece with shaking fingers and
rosined string -
the throbbing chain of many deep notes
no eyes are left unveiled, nor unheard

softly into the air it hangs it seeps
into the faded murals
the wooden floorboards
his lids are closed and trembling
with the sweetened, saddened tone

a rise, a rise
and one rises choking up
falling with his fists
lush velour deep-hanging drapery

ancient song plays a
lone caresser
at last the living silence
at long last

with abounding vibrato

-LH

The Asylum Seekers

Whatever you did and did not do was done and not to me.

If you took the shirts off their backs, you divided my own clothing.

If you did not care for them in prison, you neglected me.

If you broke their fingers, you hurt my hand that was wounded for your sake.

If you strangled them, you cut off the breath of my holy life.

If you did not offer refuge, you did not reach out to me.

If you sent them to be killed, you gave me over to be killed.

They are my own brothers; don't doubt that I will love and keep them.

They will be some of the brightest jewels in my crown of triumph.

And if you say to me, Lord, Lord, I will say: Look what you did to me.

-HSK

Bear All Things

For You, Lord, the loveliest

You, the prime of love, of light

You, beatitude, delight

You, incomprehensible

You, the face of beauty, bliss,

You, the final godsend, gift

For You, Lord, we'll bear all things.

Glory to the spring of strength.

-HSK

Coteleworker

It looks so warm, this feline form,
Dozing cozy in the sun.
He feeds on fish, a pungent dish,
Gazing lazy at the street.
I work all day, he gets to play,
Napping happy when he wants.
It's not fair, this lump of hair,
Leading greedy all nine lives.

-HSK

Saltbush Lives Forever

Memories
Of earthy saltbush
In the mouth
Bounded by
A bowl of baked-dust blue on
The land's crazed clay plate-

They're too much.
There's too much gladness,
Too much grief
At the past
Passing, that home being cast
Aside, callously

By grown-ups
Who moved on with life.
Yes, but now
We know God
Who assures: none of this flawed-
Seeming life is waste.

That brushland
With all its barren
Breathing room
Eternally
Is a part of what will be
What built me into

A living

Laborer for my

Redeemer.

The desert

Is deathless, through Christ in me,

Through Christ's work in me.

-HSK

Tinsel Prophet

Her eyes catch
And hold on the flecks
Of prisms
Thrown off by
The rings and recessed lights like
Private festivals.

The guests pause
To watch and wonder,
Uneasy,
What's made her
So solemn as if dazzled
By some great omen.

The answer's
In her paperweights
And crystal.
They think her
Prophetic- but, more mundane,
She's charmed by glitter.

-HSK

Milk Leaps

The silver rod slips into place

Fluorescent glimmer of singing bulbs

Shimmers across hills of cotton blossoms

Beyond, feet tap rhythm under grinning harmony

Milk leaps black from white folds of skin

A heart beats itself in softened time

Life curls in a rosy spiral

And tastes the salt ecstasy of loneliness

-HSK

Swampland

That little roadside bit of soggy swamp-
No wonder things like alligators thrive.
The Lord never finished
Lifting this piece of land from the sea;
Half-lifted and half-formed,
Primeval horrors
Thrive here because it's
Partial.

But heaven needs the grimness of a swamp.
This jumbled wonder couldn't fully thrive
If He ever finished
Lifting this piece of land from the sea.
I love the cold, clean plains-
But in this fertile
Frightful grove there is
Fullness.

-HSK

Guilty By Reason of Inattention

And here's another guilt to add

To the jumbled drawer of tedious guilts

That rummage themselves, announce themselves

And their companions in the waiting spaces

Between a greeting and a joke.

Of course you were manifestly absent-

Electrically so- the spaces extended

By seconds and seconds and seconds-

The stench of cigarettes in smokeless air-

The jerk of the wheel alibied as another haha trick,

Scared you, didn't I? You thought for one space

That I was wrestling alone a roaring blankness- nah.

Frightened oblivion laughed and went into hiding,

And we laughed, too, you space cadet.

You introvert retreating into your sequestered skull

In the middle of the family holiday,

Until the wreck and your skull adorned with a party's worth

Of colored ribbons wrapped up the obvious

And handed it over with- hah- thumbs up.

A childhood constellation of empty spaces

Resolved grimly into a figure

Of two decades' absentminded laughter

With no salvation offered.

-HSK

(Untitled)

When sleep slipped through my exhaustion

like wind I cannot catch

flitting and weaving just out of my reach,

I used to think of you

I dreamed you beside me

with my eyes wide open

Your arms around me

kept me safe from the night

safe from the world

safe from myself

Wrapped in your offering,

whether you were there or not,

finally, I slept.

When my mind slipped through my heart

like panicked lightning bolts

I tried to shut it out

I told it that it did not belong there

and I dreamed you there instead,

trying to let your love -

offered up wholly and holy and without withholding -

ease my fear, be enough,

quiet the terror in my veins.

When I slipped through your fingers
like breath you cannot hold onto,
my hair beyond your reach,
my touch too light upon your skin,
I cried out for the loss of
the rescue that took my breath away
My heart beat hard and then died,
finally overwhelmed by my mind and my nerves
I tried to dream you into me, but I failed.

I wanted to say yes with every bit of my soul
but I ran like a child into the night.

-LH

The Universal Hymn

If, on the off chance, you have prayed for visions
You didn't even know how to describe in asking
And, gone to bed too late again, you're answered
With a stunning blow that crumbles your darkly spectral rock
And leaves a circle in the wall of your soul
Through which the entire universe is visible
In points of gaslight giving off fiery music
Into the soft, supporting, surrounding darkness
(Unflagging vehemence of song,
Abiding mildness of the immaculate
Listening infinity)
And everything, all life, unknowingly calling
One great hymn in harmony out to the eternal
Silence-
Okay, turn over, rub your face against the pillow's
Pleasing sleekness, and wander off into the
Arid tedium of your brain's dreams again.
Why you get given what you ask for is beyond me,
But now you know- it is well is not a lie-
And you'll have the waking daytime to deal
With the gaping wound you asked for.

-HSK

124

Jaelynn

She came bursting in on our desert lives
As a clean brooklet springing from the rock
Gravely- that, or merrily- courteous-
Depending on the day's circumstances.
Little waterfall woman, with bare feet
In the icy stream, learning to skip rocks-
With our hearts in our throats for the question:
How far to tip the scale toward freedom?
If she went over, we'd be destitute-
With no answer for how we lost the girl
With ancient humor in her rainy eyes.
When she left the water with dripping hem
To answer the photographer's beckon,
We watched her pick her way over pinecones
With our unease easing into rawness-
Because a new child brings a freshness
With a fearful vulnerability.

-HSK

Song of a Woman

I am
a woman who knows herself -
my strength and my softness
my determination and my love

I have grown
and I am growing
by myself
or in the knowing
of someone else, but no matter what -
I will always
always
continue to grow taller
and rounder in my knowledge
of myself
I will never stop learning

I will cry when it hurts
I will keep company with pain,
giving it my quiet presence
until it is done
I will sing when I want
celebrating life
I welcome the sun each morning:
Bring it on!

I wear my soul on the outside
like this
It lets me feel everything,
and feeling everything,

I am enormous

If my soul out here benefits you,

help yourself,

as I am love and life and joy and light and pain and sorrow and celebration,

but I will let no one strip me of me

and I mean

no one.

-LH

Center

Meanwhile,
At the center
Of everything, a well
Of the clearest water sits in
Mourning.

-HSK